Ax

Flashlight

Mask

Fire Extinguisher

STOP

Stop Sign

Safety Vest

Walkie-Talkie

Helmet

Headlamp

D1403768

"When I was a boy and I would see scary
things in the news, my mother would say to me,
'Look for the helpers. You will always find
people who are helping.'"

—Fred Rogers

For Tien and Reid

All rights reserved. Published in the United States by Random House
Children's Books, a division of Penguin Random House LLC, New York.

Random House and the colophon are registered trademarks of Penguin Random House LLC.

Visit us on the Web! rhcbooks.com

Educators and librarians, for a variety of teaching tools, visit us at RHTeachersLibrarians.com

Library of Congress Cataloging-in-Publication Data is available upon request.
ISBN 978-1-5247-6562-0 (trade) — ISBN 978-1-5247-6563-7 (lib. bdg.) —
ISBN 978-1-5247-6564-4 (ebook)

MANUFACTURED IN CHINA
10 9 8 7 6 5 4 3 2 1
First Edition

HOORAY FOR HELPERS!

First Responders and More Heroes in Action

MIKE AUSTIN

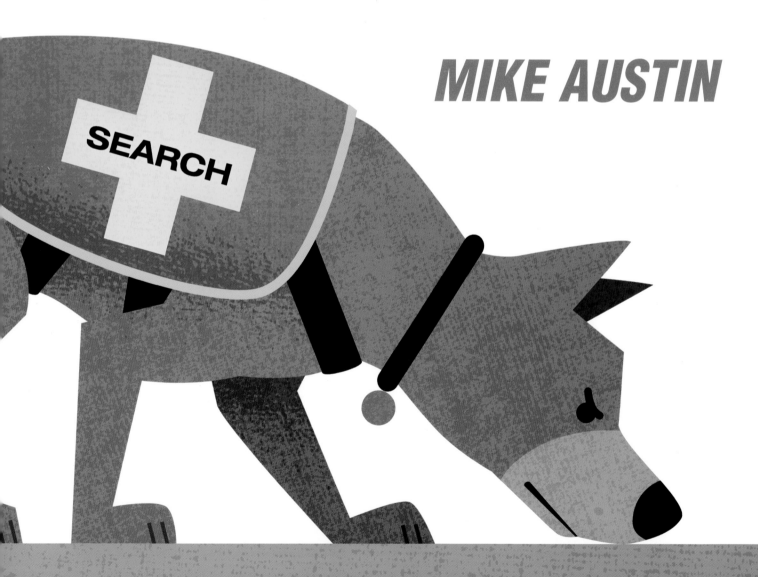

Random House 🏠 New York

Who is a first responder?

They can be firefighters, police officers, school nurses, doctors, and other helpers who lend a hand.

"911!"

When they get the call,
they jump into action!

THEY ARE THE FIRST TO

HELP IN AN EMERGENCY.

They watch over big cities . . .

Ambulance

Gurney

Police Officer

Fire Hydrant

Fire Hose

Fire Engine

Tow Truck

CHARLIE'S CHATTY CHICKENS

. . . and small towns.

Crane

Traffic
Sign

Stop
Sign

STOP

ROAD
CLOSED

Chain Saw

POWER & LIGHT Co.

First responders are ready all day . . .

Headlamp

Boom Lift

Electric Company Truck

POWER & LIGHT Co.

Safety Barrier

and all night.

They keep alert by the shore.

Lifeguard Station

Binoculars

Whistle

CAUTION
STRONG
CURRENTS
BEWARE!

SURF RESCUE

Rescue
Board

Rappelling
Rope

Search and
Rescue Diver

. . . and high up in the sky.

WHOOSH!

Water

These helpers brave any kind of weather.

Life Jacket

Helmet

Raft

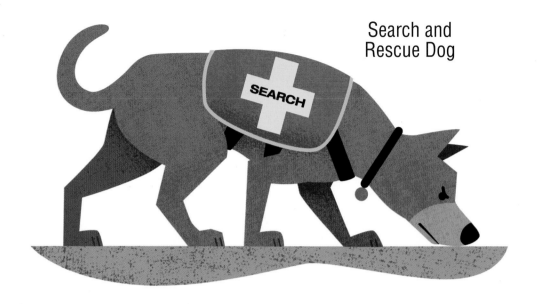

Search and
Rescue Dog

Police Horse

They also join forces with animal friends.

Capuchin
Monkey Helper

Emergency
Supplies

Blanket

Volunteer
Aid Worker

National Guard

WATER WATER WATER WATER WATER WATER WATER WATER WATER WATER WATER WATER WATER WATER WATER WATER WATER WATER WATER WATER

Fresh Water

When many people need them, helpers are there.

Poncho

WATER WATER

First Aid
Kit

They are there when just one calls for help.

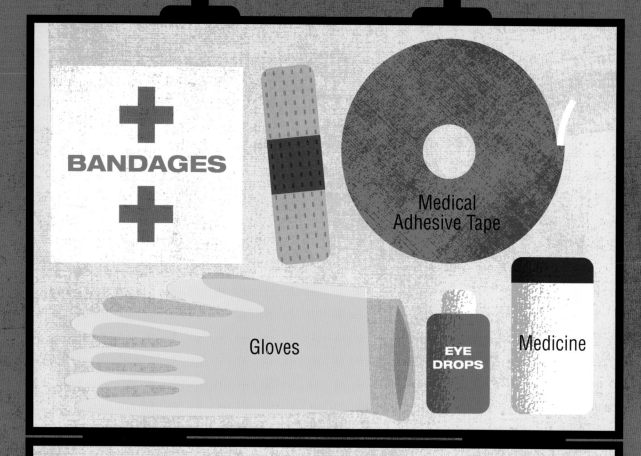

BANDAGES

Medical
Adhesive Tape

Gloves

EYE
DROPS

Medicine

OINTMENT

Antiseptic
Wipes

Splinter
Tweezers

Gauze Pads

Scissors

Bandage

They keep everyone safe.

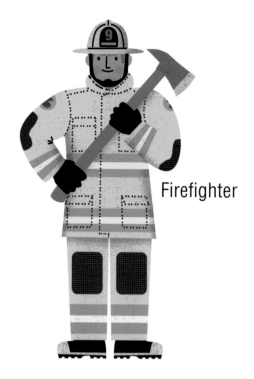
Firefighter

Police Officer

Doctor

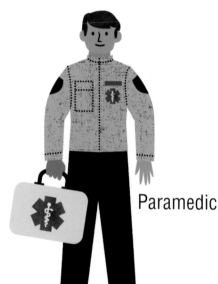
Paramedic

They are real-life superheroes.

Lifeguard

Coast Guard
Pilot

Red Cross
Volunteer

Ski
Patroller
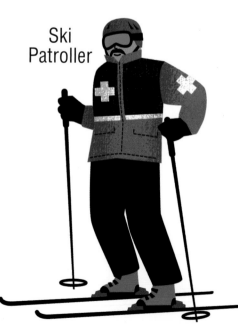

National
Guard
Soldier

911 Emergency
Dispatcher

Smoke
Jumper

Teacher

For everything you do, "THANK YOU, FIRST RESPONDERS!"

School
Counselor

School
Security
Guard

School
Nurse

School
Crossing
Guard

Hello there! My name is Anthony, and I'm a firefighter in New York City. Do you have any questions for me?

ASK A REAL FIREFIGHTER!

How did you train to be a firefighter?
There is a training school called the fire academy. The program lasts several months and teaches the ins and outs of the job. There is an academic component and lots of hands-on simulations, such as putting out fires, climbing ladders, and sliding down ropes on the outside of a building.

What's your favorite part of your job?
The people I work with. The closest friendships of my life have been formed in the firehouse.

How much does your equipment weigh?
At *least* a hundred pounds. In addition to the bunker gear, this includes tools like hooks, saws, hoses, and a mask.

Do you go down a pole, like in the movies?
I do, but I prefer the stairs. I usually throw my shoes down the pole hole and walk downstairs.

How many fires have you put out?
I don't really keep count—maybe I should! I've been to many fires, some big and some small, and they were *all* put out.

Have you ever rescued a dog or a cat?
Nope, but some of my friends have!

Is it hard being a firefighter?
It *can* be hard, both physically and emotionally. But helping people is rewarding and outweighs the challenges.

Do you get scared?
I do, but working with my friends helps calm me down.

How important is teamwork to you?
It is important. Working as a team is the only way a fire will go out and the only way we get to go home safely.

How can someone become a first responder?
It depends on the path you choose. But if you're interested in becoming a firefighter, you should go to your local firehouse and ask how. (Just avoid dinner and nap time!)

HELP YOUR FAMILY BUILD AN EMERGENCY KIT!
Collect these items, and keep them together in a safe place.

EMERGENCY SUPPLIES

- Three-day supply of nonperishable food (dried fruit, canned food, peanut butter, etc.)

- Three-day supply of water—at least a gallon per person for each day

- First aid kit (with essential medications)

- Can opener

- Paper plates and cups, plastic utensils, paper towels

- Trash bags

- Flashlight with extra batteries

- Sleeping bag or blanket for everyone in your family

- Three-day supply of clothes, including sturdy shoes. (Consider the weather where you live.)

- Matches in a waterproof container. (Only grown-ups should handle these!)

- Books, games, or puzzles

- Toothbrushes, toothpaste, soap

- Battery-powered or hand-cranked radio with extra batteries

- Cell phone with an extra battery and a solar charger

- Whistle to signal for help

- Local maps

- Pet supplies

Visit **ready.gov/kids** for more information, activities, and games!

Grab a piece of paper, and make a list of numbers you can call in an emergency. Put the list up where you can always see it. Here's what to include!

EMERGENCY CONTACT LIST
IN CASE OF EMERGENCY, CALL 911

- Your family name
- Your home address
- Your home phone number
- Neighbor's name
- Relative's name

- Family doctor
- Police dept.
- Fire dept.
- Ambulance

Ask an adult for help, and look for *Hooray for Helpers!* on rhcbooks.com. There, you'll find a printable version of this list, which you can fill in with your own contacts.

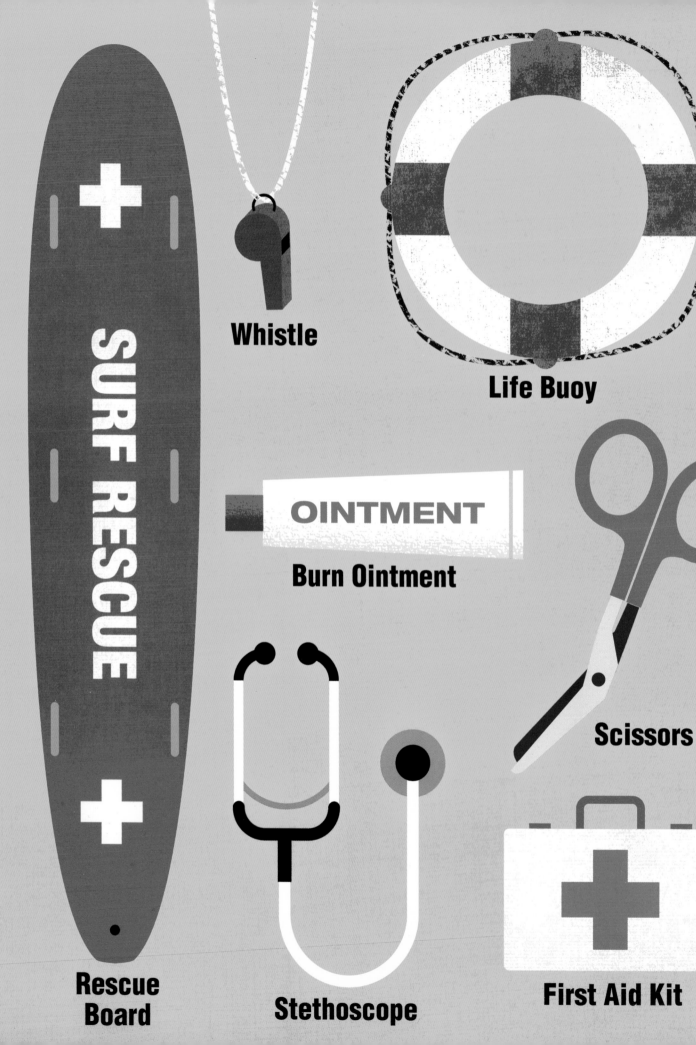

Whistle

Life Buoy

OINTMENT

Burn Ointment

Scissors

Rescue Board

Stethoscope

First Aid Kit

SURF RESCUE